Reverend Clayton:
"You wanna quit, Ethan?"

Ethan:
"That'll be the day."

THE SEARCHERS

John Ford
(1956)

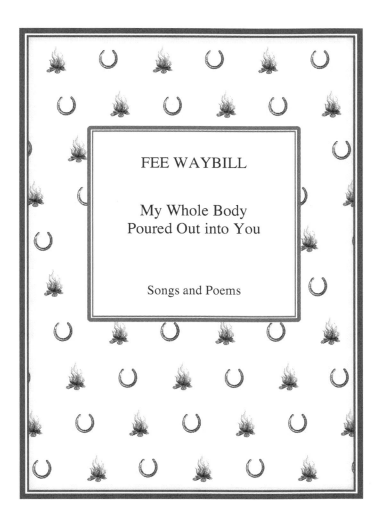

FEE WAYBILL

My Whole Body
Poured Out into You

Songs and Poems

Contents

POEMS

Around the Campfire

SONGS

Love

Hate

Lies

From This Day Forward

From this day forward
The first day of the rest of our lives
I will love you only
and keep you safe and warm and close by my side
I will hold back the darkness
and work for a future that is bright
I will give you my all
My strength my heart my love my life
From this day forward
as husband and wife
we'll outsmart our shadows
and shine as one light

March 20, 1993

POEMS

Superfee

My odes to my Lizzi Bang
seem as doomed as a man to hang
The joy of our love's caper
has evaporated into vapor
But hard as a bed of nails
the wind in my solemn sails
blows as strong as the man of steel
Because I know my love is real

Jane

The one thing in the world
most important to tell
is none but the girl
with the undeniable spell
Who walked from the jungle
to the steps of inscription
not knowing she held
my life's love prescription
And now as I ponder
the time and the tears
I wouldn't change the wonder
and I cherish the years
And the love that was born
on that solar eclipse
and the fire still so warm
that burns on my lips

Sighs from the Jungle

I make funny sighing sounds
I've never heard myself make
when I think of you and how I love you
for love's sake
It seems strange to me
I've never made these sounds before
but it's ok because it somehow adds to the
"begun in the jungle" lore

The Pirate and the Pyramid

I miss you so much
my eyes hurt from squinting
My mind's had enough
of so obvious hinting
The persistent pedantic
urgings embarrass
and border no cross
the lines that do harass
Please help me walk
from the edge of the plank
and realize all
that you've given to thank
my lucky stars that
shown so bright that night
when we met at the top
of a pyramids height
'Til words stop the wind
'Til the moon won't raise the tide
and the sun refuses to shine

Mauna Fee

More and more the magma of my soul
is bursting out of me in a love volcano
My lips tremble
My knees quake
My fingers fumble
My hands shake
I feel like my heart
is going to explode
'Til I remember that with you
I'll never be alone
again

The Cliff

As the evening puts on
it's cloak of darkness
and leads it's disciples to sleep
The love in my heart for you swells
'til I'm helpless
to turn from the cliff, and I leap
Into the night
with no bottom in sight
just love to cushion my fall
From the grace that your faith
had sustained then erased
I forever will wait for your call

Buzzard Meat

If I could only hug and kiss you again
Hope does spring eternal just a matter of when
Can't do anything can't help myself
Love you forever and ever or else
Be left for the buzzards to eat
and the sun for my bones to bleach

'Til then

I am yours 'til the end of days
'Til the blood in my veins runs cold
'Til the light from the sun fades
and the mountains crumble and fold
'Til the rivers run dry
and the oceans drain
and dragon's breath
rules the world again
'Til then

The Promise

The poignant promise of your love
sustains me
The future fulfillment is enough
to retain in me
The hope that the years
and the pain and the tears
have not all been in vain
and my madness for you doesn't drive me insane
Inspiration of my life
with a two sided knife

Wonderland

If the definition of madness
so well known
is doing the same thing over and over
and never reaping what is sown
Still then as I ask myself
what is the matter
Deep inside I know
I'm as mad as a hatter
No top hat needed
No noxious bow tie
It's as plain as my nose
Just look in my eye

Simple Pleasures

Just to hold you in my arms
a simple pleasure taken for granted
To keep you safe and warm
my soul purpose on this planet
Was so strangely found then lost
leaving just an empty husk
Never dreaming of the cost
of betraying sacred trust

Wind

What is it about you
that pulls the prose from me
Unlike anyone before or after
can ever dare to compete
I guess the only answer
is cast to restless wind
To blow to the four corners
and maybe back again
I will wait for that wind

Hope

The audacity of hope
is not only universal
but personal
The side of the slippery slope
will only get slicker
and slip quicker
If we don't bail out the boat
and cling desperately together
forever and ever
we'll never learn how to cope
so our mutual attraction
brings eternal satisfaction
Love you 'til the earth
ceases to spin

The Five Fs

I worry about you and think about you
and wish and hope and dream
I know I come across as strong
but I'm not what I seem
All in all we are so blessed
and secure in our lives
How lucky we are
I don't think we realize
Fate and faith in our future
will fulfill our fortune

The Death of Hercules

When you said we could never
get back together
you ripped the heart from my chest
forever forever
No colon close parenthesis
text symbol can weather
the trail of tears caused by your termination
of my tether

I'll never mention a word of my grief
 again to you to your relief
I'll be as succinct as
An Indian chief
Life dies and is renewed
be it ever so brief
I will attempt to be as strong
as Hercules

Another

All the odes to Lizzi I wrote
may not change my swan song
even a note
But just the knowledge
that my lyric of love
was as pure a potion
that ever was
sustains my strong affirmation of faith
and fulfills my earnest endeavor of grace
Because as sure as the day
turns to night
my heart will
never give up the fight

Poets

Does Cyrano's epic plea to Roxanne
plead my case or in any way up my hand
Does Shakespeare's Romeo understand
that Juliet's heart still loves the man
History's poets of love and loss
are heaped in a pile overgrown with moss
I fear my verses are like waves being tossed
and overturned by the crushing cost
But I won't go quietly into the night
because I love you more than the sun shines bright

Three Faces

The three faces of Eve
had nothing on you
She must have been a breeze
compared to the hoops you've made me jump through
Never wanted to believe
I was meant to be alone
But more and more I see
the lights are off and I'm still home
My heart is in spasm
beating wildly in my chest
Like I've fallen in a chasm
without a bottom broken nest

21

Who dries my tears
and stills my fears
and gives me meaning
for twenty one years
No one knows
what fate has in store
The ups and downs
the wolf at the door
I only pray
that for rich or for poor
I'm allowed to love you
for twenty one more

21 and Counting

I haven't loved you for twenty-one years
because you weren't the smartest, sexiest,
most beautiful girl in the world
So know that your hard work and perseverance
will reward you
As your life continues to unfurl
I can only hope and pray I'll be part of it
as we live, love and laugh
through our lives
in the undying dream
that you and I will again
be each others husbands and wives

Night's Breath

The cloak of the night
conceals my delight
that you are though far
still secure in my arms
and I wait in the wings
for a breath that will bring
joy back to my life
and you back to me as my wife

Hang 'em High

Just the mention of maybe maybe
has renewed my hallucination of hope
I live to fulfill the fantasy
that both our destinies can cope
with two lives that are worlds apart
But connect with a glue that is strong
that will bond together two hearts
and repair anything that goes wrong

You've set me all a flutter
My heart has turned to butter
But I'll hold my joyous anticipation in check
'til the noose that strangles me
loosens around my neck

Just Say Yes

Just say yes
one more time
Surrender to the strength
in my arms
Suspend the suspicion
I see in your eyes
But still subject to the heartstrings
of my charms
Break through the bandoliers
that entwine
and strap your breasts
from imagined harm
Just say yes one more time
and for the rest of your life
I'll keep you warm

Please Mr. Custer

We cannot love alone
Our journey is joined together
Our dream of our happy home
will need a tougher tether
And all the strength we can muster
All the muscle we can build
So we don't end up like Custer
all alone on that deadly hill
Believe in me
I believe in you

Poker Face

Whatever is left of me
is yours
I don't have the strength
to fight any more wars
I have never been able
to tell your tell
Or convince you of what's really
at the bottom of my well
And you always held
the winning hand
And I'll always be
the lonely man
But never admit to
a lesson learned
and try for redemption
from a woman spurned

That Long

I'll love you 'til death calls in his marker
and demands his pound of flesh
'Til the circus side show barker
steps right up and fails the test
'Til the river runs uphill
and the lava flow runs cold
'Til time has lost his will
and admits he's just too old
That's how long I'll love you
That's how long I'll love you

Bloodshot

I haven't seen you
for so long
My love is bleeding out my eyes
I'm a blind man
No sight no song
With just the memory of those precious nights
You are the moon of my life
The sun of my sunset
My life's one and only wife
The love I have never left

Remember Me

Remember me
No more complicated missive
than remember me
Nothing anymore impressive
than remember me
All the heartfelt invocations
that surrendered me
and the monk-like moderation
that amended me
Nothing more and nothing less
than I expect to be
Not withstanding all the mess
that's not perfect in me
Only asking this one thing
To just remember me

Around the Campfire

Friends

The rainbow bridge is calling my Harley
to reunite in the sky with his old friend Charley
To run and to play like the boys that they were
with no more pain as free as a bird
To have a big party to laugh and to sing
With Minnie and Gerry and Frosty and Lizzi Two Bang
These babies of mine I will never forget
I will love them forever
They were much more that just pets
They were friends

Mona Hunkas

The sweetest dog in the whole wide world
Was none other than my sweet Mona girl
She loved me more than the day is long
Never ever ever did anything wrong

Big brown eyes that would melt my soul
Kept the wolf from my door kept me warm in the cold
Made me so happy every day of her life
I'm still so sad I can't sleep at night

I still see the love that poured from her eyes
Even though she has crossed the rainbow bridge in the sky
I will never forget her for the rest of my life
And look forward to the day when she will be back by my side

The Horse

A cowboy is only as good as his horse
Won't be caught dead riding a mule
Keeps him tall in the saddle and true to his course
and saves him from acting the fool

Riding line or rounding 'em up
he can count on his pal not to fade
But finding a good one is more than just luck
they just don't come along everyday

And like a good woman they need lots of love
and tenderness so they don't spook
If they ever break your heart from the sky above
"That'll be the day" said The Duke

My first was Cassie and she broke the mold
Not a bone in her body wasn't right
And then there was Double very solemnly sold
She would never turn her head from a fight

Next was the man that was pulled from the ashes
Cadillac is the leader of the pack
Then Maya who was so big her mom still has flashes
but she begs to have me on her back

Sinatra was without a doubt the best of them all
Ran with the wind in his hair
But his hopes were cut short by an ugly fall
and life lame in a pasture just ain't fair

There's not been a cowboy blessed with such flesh
and a day don't go by I don't give thanks
I'll be happy I had them to my last dying breath
and you can take that partner to the bank

One Eyed Jack

Left me here to rot
A tub of guts was all I got
Five years in a hole
killing time growing old

But something deep inside
kept talking to me
I won't forget those nights
not as long as I breathe

I'm a one-eyed jack
I don't shoot straight
Hide the other side of my face
So don't look back
cause you got no time
for a pack of lies

That's my sad tale
Worth a gob of spit and a rusty nail
But it's not my style
to shed a tear and cry awhile

So don't think bad about
me cause I'm gone
I can't help running out
that's the way I was born

I know what you think
You're probably right
But that don't change a thing
I can't change my sights

Senorita Don't Say No

Lost my money beaten bloody
lost my rolling rodeo
Seen the glamour I've seen the slammer
had it up to here with rock and roll

But I think I've found the answer
to repossess my life
Just slip below the border
and make a dark eyed woman my wife

Senorita don't say no
You're my last chance
and you know how I love Mexico
Senorita don't say no
cause I've got no place left to go

Loved a redhead left a brunette
and I always had a thing for blonds
I knew the big names I talked a good game
for a little fish in a great big pond

But it's time to make my exit
and I think I see the light
It's not as though I'm desperate
but it looks like I'll be leaving tonight

What's become of the quiet heroes
Marlon Brando Steve McQueen
Up to this point my life's a zero
but I'll be big on the Spanish screen

Spur of the Moment

Sometimes it's better if you answer
on the spur of the moment
Sometimes it's better if you just
don't think about it too long

Before you analyze the consequences
say what's inside your heart and take your chances
right or wrong

Save the why   it's no good
Save the where   it won't help
Keep the wonder what I'm doing here
to yourself
Unannounced   not a word
Unprepared   aren't we all
Suddenly true love is there
and we fall

Sometime we make our best decisions
on the spur of the moment
Cause while you're thinking something
beautiful could walk out the door

You have to shiver when the feeling shakes you
Could find forever in the time it takes to
cross the floor

The bad news is
it's no use counting to ten
The best trick is
move quick
cause you never know when love will hit you again

One Fifty One

Pay your money take your shot
Just remember
dead men lay where they drop
Take your chances slim and none
You'll be crucified before you've begun

I might take all you have to give
and you'll be lucky if you live

One fifty one's more fun
than punching time the same old grind
One fifty one's more fun
than being broke without a joke to sell
One fifty one's more fun
than salty tears and watered beers
One fifty one's more fun
than hating life without a wife to tell

Buy your ticket stand in line
Do you think you
could be more blind
Make your choices weave your web
and you wonder
why you wish you were dead

You might not get the chance again
You better take it while you still can

Cowboys and Dreamers

Once upon a time
with an innocence so fair
In the good old days of black and white
when we lived without a care

Things will never be the same
only got ourselves to blame
Can't help yearning for those days
Those days of yore

When our heroes all wore cowboy hats
and the good guys always won
The bad guys always dressed in black
and it seemed the world was young

Johnny Yuma to The Cisco Kid
or The Rifleman's on the way
Didn't matter what the villain did
they would always save the day

I want to go back then
I still remember when
The Lone Ranger rides again
and the mask he wore

But now who's gonna hear my plea
Who's going to send the cavalry
I guess it's only in my dreams
My dreams and nothing more

SONGS

Love

As Time Turns the Page

As the leaves bare the trees
and never know their sin
You and me only reaching
then scattered by the wind

Nothing lost you have to find
No defense for a state of mind
short of saying so long and wondering why

You left my heart in a cloud of dust
Now only memories are waiting for us
But if I just hold on
Pain turns to long gone
As time turns the page

Looking back with the chance
I wouldn't change a thing
Checkered past everlasting
beyond my wildest dreams

Stolen lifetimes in the dark
No regrets for a broken heart
and no delusions of love sent from afar

Still there's harsh reminder
with every step I take
The truth won't be denied
or neatly tucked away
But time will turn the page

Find Your Way

I've got a remedy
You get the first one free
It should be all you need
to follow

It just takes half the time
It doesn't cost a dime
I think it's lightning
in a bottle

Just break the looking glass you're fastened to
and stay the darkness shining through

No magic wand
divining rod
nobody's wind up god
will find your way
No golden road
or potion sold
no ancient secret code
can find your way
Your way to me

You say you lost at love
Cashed out and given up
and nobody to call your bluff
belated

I'll turn your inside out
Lost lovers finally found
Stop having to walk around
sedated

You might be innocent and alone
and I might be guilty all alone
But I'll stop the river raining down your tears
and I'd say it's only up from here

From this Day

No one would ever know
no one but me and you
We could go on with our lives
and this would be through
Holding you here beside me
I could turn back the morning sun
All that I thought I had
seems like a world without reason

I really ought to go
but your lips tell me to stay
Take me away

From this day life begins
Nothing that came before
gave me more
From this day love forgives
all the mistakes we made
on our way to this day

How will we know tomorrow
what the shadows can see tonight
Only as one shall we stand
ever as brave in the light

You ask me not to go
You say it right from your soul
Now I know

Ask for my strength
Ask for my heart
Everything I thought was gone
was waiting just for you to come along

Hold Out Your Hand

Hold out your hand
the window to the master plan
Hold out the other
see what you can uncover

And you'll be revealed to me
the dark and forgotten places
Illuminating mystery
identifying strange faces

Hold out your hand
I can make you understand
Hold out the other
I can help you discover

Don't be afraid to see
the hidden reflection
A look into infinity
to strengthen your direction

Just hold out your hand

Rest Your Worries on Me

Feeling lonely
Not the only thing I'm sure
you could show me
when you told me how to cure

Trouble always stands twice as high
when you're looking up alone
We could cut it down to size
and maybe leave the dog a bone

I'm ready
I'm willing
You're not the only one you're killing
Rest your worries on me
and watch them disappear
I'm willing
I'm able
I'm sitting at an empty table
Rest your worries on me
and wash away your tears

Never know how
we could work out
Two as one
Think it's time now
Think we find out
All or none

Can you put your love on the line
with nothing left to give
Like a matching bookend to mine
We'll only just begin to live

You'd be surprised how quickly they fade
Like rumors on the wind
I can whisper your worries away
before they begin

Stand or Fall

I close my eyes at night
and imagine arms around me
I can almost taste your kiss
I'm looking for the sky
where the shooting stars
put out the lights
cause I know what to wish

Anyway anywhere
anytime you need me I'll be there
Night or day
I'll be waiting for your call
Anything anyhow
any moment and I'm starting now
Stand or fall
Stand or fall

I see the morning's glow
and the rays of light renew me
I know there's nothing out of reach
Another day unfolds
with the possibility it holds
and I can't wait to see

It's not a case of right or wrong
it's just the way it is
I've got to find another way to live

Single by Night

You would never guess
Flawless in appearance
Fashionable dress
Knock you to your knees
All the self assurance
he could ever need
They can't help but drool
Flawless in appearance
Fabulously cool
So hard to believe
All the self assurance
I know he's really

Single by night
Hopelessly alone and
staring at the four walls
Single by night
Desperately single
Desperately waiting
Still single single by night

No chance will escape
He's constantly pursuing
every pretty face
Comic tragedy
Nothing so amusing
nothing left but sadly

The daylight conceals the true story
The night will reveal the real one

Talking to the Moon

When the cool winds blow
and the light decides to fade
I can feel the flow
like a drug inside my veins
And I can't stand still
not hard to understand
it takes all my will
to remember who I am
Oh darling I don't wonder why
and it doesn't matter don't matter how I try
Now it's almost dark and I feel so all alone
but I got nowhere to run to I'm still hanging on

She's got me talking to the moon
Got no one else to talk to
She's got me talking to the moon
Cause I can't get over you, talking to the moon
She's got me talking to the moon
Don't want to talk to myself, talking to the moon
She's got me talking to the moon
Cause I can't get over you

And in the midnight dawn
when the sky begins to glow
I can hear the call
like a beat inside my soul
And 'til the break of day
I'll be talking to that man
Cause I've lost my way
and I don't know who I am
Oh darling I'll hit the road
I see your signs but I still don't know which way to go
And when the cool winds blow with the answer on it's breath
on that day you'll hear me and we will love again

What If

What if the worst of things were really true
What if the sky was really falling
What if those words I do were only for show
What if I never really know

What if it's just a test I've got to take
What if it only makes me stronger
What if it only takes the rest of my life
What if you come back home tonight

On my ship of fools
there isn't any room to wonder
It's a lonely way to live
but this is all I have to give
Don't want to think about what if

What if I set the clock for yesterday
What if the teardrops were forgotten
What if we found a way to fall in love again
What if we found another chance

Thought that I'd already done
my share of wishing
Looking for the time when wishing won
and we can get back to kissing

Whenever You Cry

A true love
tender touch
more that I ever dreamed
All came true
wrapped in you
gave me my fantasy

I've only waited all of my life
Now the waiting is done

Whatever happens you're the one
It's like all the stars have aligned
I see the dreamer through the disguise
I'll wipe the tears from your eyes
Whenever you cry

Reach too far
leave a scar
nothing that I couldn't heal
Feel the rush
learn to trust
all that you're aching to feel

You've only waited all of your life
Now there's no reason to run

Someday we'll look back
and smile at the thought
Somehow we conquered our fear
Something inside us
we could have lost
Now it seems so very clear

Woulda Coulda Shoulda

Monday morning quarterbacks
are Tuesday's memory
Only hit a thousand for a day

Not so many fish to catch
if you can't see the sea
I think I let the big one get away

Hesitated way too long
to pull the trigger now you're gone

Woulda been wonder and it
coulda been thunder
You could see the lightning hanging low
Shoulda been heaven rolling
seven eleven
But my luck ran out the dice were cold

Looked to Nostradamus for
an answer from the past
But there was no solution to my plight

Somehow Doubting Thomas
doesn't seem the one to ask
Guess I'll still be spending lonely nights

There is no one left to call
Only breath to break the fall

Esperanza

I'm afraid to dream
Afraid of what I dream
might mean
Afraid that I might come apart
at the seams
Cause I'm only just a scared
human being

Then I wake up and see the sparking sea
and I realize how lucky
I am to be me
A brand new day
alive and free
Me and my baby
and the swaying palm trees

Happy and sad comedy and tragedy
life's interwoven
fabric of fantasy
Day lives for night
and night for the moonbeams
I live for Lizzi
and dreams are just dreams

Hate

Another Think Coming

I'm not too old to figure it out
I still remember my youth
I know I still know the language
Won't be long 'til I'm back in the groove

I'm going to need some practice
It might take a couple of tries
I might even have some questions
but I'll eventually get it right

I bet you think I lay awake at night
all blue and black and all through
You probably think I've quit without a fight
but you've got another think coming to you

I'm moving fast now baby
You call I'm out on the town
I'll be cruising down the main drag
doing my best just to tear it down

Heart attack could come tomorrow
So who are you holding tonight
Don't want to be safe or sorry
Just trying to take a big bite

Blow You Away

I've scuffled around
and I've never been no one's fool
Surprised what I found
Gotta blow you away
How do you know
when you stumbled in love
Wait for the blood to show
or let it blow you away
Even a fool can see that something's wrong
Singing the blues can only play so long

Not dumb as you guess
I can see the facade I bought
But I'm swelling my chest
to let it blow me away
Leaving my lonely
Gotta walk the line
I gotta release those lips
Before they blow me away

Make the same mistake a second time
isn't any bolder
Make the same mistake a third time
You're only getting older
Make the same mistake until you die
Some would call it crazy
Make the same mistake another lie
Blowing you away

I'm packing my life
and the speck of respect I've left
They say love is blind
It'll blow you away
You could call it a crime
Love in the first degree
You could say that I've done my time
While it blows you away

But You'll Remember

If you find it hard to tell
the daylight from the dream
it might just be another toxic symptom
It ain't no magic spell
no cosmic laser beam
It might just be a crucial lack of wisdom

You've been chasing your fortune for years
Had an ace up your short sleeve shirt
Now you're surprised that you're cards disappeared
It's a drag but the truth hurts

Cause the time rushes by like a leaf on the wind
cast with no path or direction and then
leaving no trace that it ever has been
Death to the right and the wrong
Don't know what you've got 'til it's gone
but you'll remember

If you think there's something more
there's a shadow of a doubt
You've got just one more thing to figure out

Faker

Your never mind is never ending
Ever ready answers on your lips
You bring new meaning to pretending
I'm waiting for the hangman's knot to slip

Don't know how you justify the fraud
Love like that should be against the law

Wipe that smile right off your face
You used up your saving grace
And I confess I've finally learned
only so much soul will burn
Choke back all that sugar and spice
Make believe you're true to life
I know it now the joke's on me
You're a faker in the first degree

Something about this seems familiar
You made a career of living lies
And you're going to find time the avenger
will show the truth to your lying eyes

One by one the spinning plates slow down
You gave up the greasepaint for the crowd

How Dare You

I don't know if it's just your style
to mix the molten with the wile
It seems to me a dangerous game
to feed the fire then fan the flame

You never know just what's in store
Be careful what you wish for

How dare you dare me not to love you
How dare you dare me to be wrong
Wonder what you'll be thinking when the blood cools
and you realize that I'm really gone

You're no stranger to the ploy
to melt the man then bait the boy
A system based on past success
that lumps me loser like the rest

I can live without the intrigue
You'll have to live without me

Hide, run and hide
Put some blinkers on your eyes
Cause the lies inside the lies
Will leave you blind

I'll take a pass on the drama
You kicked my ass with the trauma

Life is Pain

Pain is my loyal companion
I'm on a runaway train
Drive me to the edge of the canyon
Rage against the sane in my brain

Pain is the part of the story
hiding in the obvious lie
Try to find the fame and the glory
Hate to open up your blind eye

And who
do you believe
And love goes along with the rain
And life is pain

Pain keeps me on the ragged edge
I don't have the time to relax
Slide into the doubting and the dread
Twist the knife that's stuck in my back
And who
do you believe
And love goes along with the rain
And life is pain

And who
do you believe
And love goes
Along comes the pain
and tears fall like rain

Falling like rain, falling like rain, falling like rain
Falling like rain, falling like rain, falling like rain

Life is
Life
Life is pain

No Sleepless Nights

Fool to my fears
Just another old cliché
How long 'til I realize
More tears
wouldn't wash away the pain
Must have had dirt in my eye

I know it took a lot for you to say
And I just stood and watched you drive away

No sleepless nights will torture me
cause I'm waking up to you
I'll find someone to share my dreams
and tell my troubles to
No sleepless nights will torture me
cause I'm finally seeing through
your thin façade of fantasy
and I've gotten over you

How could I know
know that you were masquerading
I saw what I wanted to see
And though
though your cheap disguise is fading
Looks like the joke is on me

It sounds so funny I can't help but laugh
Now you're just something that I lost in the past

You tore my world apart
Then drove it straight through my heart

Perfect Strangers

Didn't bother with the conversation
Didn't have to try to chat you up
Let's get down to the action baby
call your bluff

I don't need to hear your whole life story
I can do without a pack of lies
I've got a four letter feeling
and not in my eyes

Wasn't one in a million reasons
It was only a thrill because it was new

You could be too good to be true
You may leave me black and blue
Fatal attraction in my face
As we cut right to the chase
Nothing that I can do
You're the perfect stranger too

We might offer love a brand new meaning
Write the secret chapter in the book
You could reveal how you learned
to hide the hook

Never know what will come tomorrow
Better take what you beg or borrow today

Goodbye, nice to know you
It's been swell
I'll write
a letter from hell

Say Goodbye

And I always wondered
what moved a moment
in ways unexpected
Resolved to be staying
next day disdaining
all I protected
My dream of love is denied
without ever closing my eyes

Say goodbye one last time
Say goodbye you're not mine
It's over it's over
Say goodbye in the dark
Say goodbye broken heart
It's over it's over now

So I'll be escaping
cause I won't be replacing
love for affection
And I'll live with the sorrow
cause it's better than borrow
love from reflection
Finally so blind that I see
that I'm the one kidding me

I've only got so much time
to forget what I waited for

Who Said That Life Was Fair

The best of intentions
will get you just that
a sickly grin and an empty hand
And crying out loud won't help
or blaming it on someone else
Just take your medicine like a man

Cause who said that life was fair
I can't remember
And don't ask me why I care
cause I can't tell you

The more you want it
the further it gets
It disappears like a distant mirage
Cause trying too hard's no good
As useless as knocking on wood
Just bite the bullet and bite it hard

You don't believe me I know
It's not my problem
If you're from Missouri
I'll show you once again

Lies

Abandon Ship

The mother of exiles said
give me your tired your poor
huddled masses.

Come into the land of the dead
but don't let the golden door
kick your asses

Our children are homeless
Our chickens are boneless
You can bring your own sacred cow

It's a new inquisition
with still the missionary position
but at least to our god you don't bow

You'd better abandon ship
before you reach our teeming shore
You'd do best to abandon ship
and go back to your land of yore
You should probably abandon ship
at least you'll be breathing free
Last chance to abandon ship
and let the tempest toss you at sea

Caveman in a Condo

Time and tide's
never gonna wait to realize
Wise guys
have petrified our fate

Only just a matter of cash
Our future's become our past

Wasteland living like a caveman in a condo
Or the spaceman sending out a message in a bottle

Greed view
and visions of a grand utopia
Seen through
and you don't understand

Someone lost the answer we had
We better find it fast

Cause the caveman's living in a condo
Thinking 'bout the
spaceman sending a message in a bottle

How if death is certain
can we keep going through the motions
without knowing what we do
We're through

We're fucked
We counted on the bridge to nowhere
Too much
has crucified the kids

Isn't time to ponder the crash
it's time to save our ass

The Everchanging Man

Running in the dark
He searches for a missing part
to fill the hole
Find the hole

Unannounced a stranger comes
and shows himself as danger from
beyond
A nameless world beyond

Trying to find a face
for the everchanging man
If he only knew the truth
he still would never understand
Trying to see the face
of the everchanging man
But his empty eyes grow silent
A cold stare in the end

Haunted by a vacant past
and clinging to the very last
The last shred of hope
that is left

Going with no place to go
Followed with no one to follow
He dances without
innocence

She can save your life in time
It's the only chance you'll find

Guns in the Holy Land

Slave to the ruling class
Grist for the mill
How could they grow so fast
Were they born to kill

Well I'm just a casual observer
Don't know what I'm talking about
but I got the word from the horse's mouth
He said there's

Guns in the holy land
Blood is in the air
Guns in the holy land
and no one even cares

How can the common man
do what is right
Fight for the promise land
but fight on which side

Cause it's just a ball of confusion
Don't know what is going on
Don't know what to do but to go along
And still there's

Guns in the holy land
Blood is in the air
Guns in the holy land
and no one even cares

And the sun never sets
unbroken
And the sons of the men
will walk these roads again

It's Only Money

I got your message
I caught my breath
I thought it sounded like
you caught your death
Are you bleeding
Have you suffered a loss
You sounded so upset
I can't imagine the cause

Don't leave me on the edge of my seat
What can it be you look fine to me

It's only money
That's no big deal
We're not curing cancer
or re-inventing the wheel
Haven't saved the whales
Didn't fix the ozone
Still playing war
with GI Joe clones
It's only money
Root of all sin
It's not going to help you get into heaven

I should be used to this
It's nothing new
Could be the masochist
inside I never knew
It keeps my life exciting
A rollercoaster ride
And just like Johnny Cash
I'm just gonna walk the line

Love Line

I caught your number on the personal page
You like to party you're all the rage
You were a time bomb
I was another john

I got your e-mail and I couldn't believe
You liked my vibe and you wanted to meet
I bought the whole song
but there was something wrong

I didn't get it initially
I don't regret it regardlessly

I found my baby on the love line
She's a mystery in real time
Then I finally realized the truth
Just thought that I was doing good with you

You have no preference and you have no shame
I'd be surprised if you remembered my name
You were a class act
that didn't talk back

Promise Land

Fat cat break your back
give us all a heart attack
Dear John money's gone
Played you for a Ponzi pawn
Mean streets talk is cheap
everybody dips their beak
Bad debts no regrets
kiss my ass and don't forget

Peace love and the white hippy dove
was a long time ago

Rub it in my face
All the rich getting richer
Holster full of mace
on the bitch getting bitchier
No one you can trust
who will ever take a stand
It's a world of dot com
and we're selling out the promise land

Drug wars oily shores
building to the perfect storm
Eating lead planet's dead
shoot yourself right in the head
What about the housing crash
What about the burn and slash
What about the hopes and dreams
Only fools would still believe

It's not fate and it's not too late
but it's getting close

I only wish this rant
was preaching to the choir
and I'm afraid one man
can never stop the fire

River of Lies

Thought I was walking on water
'til I fell in
I fell under the water
and I could not swim
I was pulled to the bottom
and I thought I would die
Then I opened my eyes
and saw the river of lies

Don't even waste your time
holding your breath
You're just a body on a beach
they haven't rescued yet
But they say one day
you'll be the front of the line
while you're floating away
on the river of lies

River of lies
We're drowning in a
river of lies
Surrounded and up to our eyes
in a river of lies

It won't even notice the tears
All those before disappeared
Another wave on the shore
Nowhere dry anymore

Sid

We all remember
the one that changed the game
Return to sender
the pleasure and the pain
Crossed the boundary
Opened up the door
Walked the ground we
never walked before
No pretender
Did not play the part
And no defenders
shot right through the heart
Young and tender
dead before he started

Didn't want to be a jukebox hero
Didn't want to be a superstar
Wasn't all about a great big ego
Wasn't all about who you are
Just a story bout a lonely kid named Sid

Tricked to trading
the high life for the high
Fate to fading
plucked right from the sky
He did it his way
Walked right up the stair
Up to the last day
never ducked a dare
He tried evading the
flotsam from the flash
Reduced to scraping
the treasure from the trash
There's no escaping
the cresting from the crash

Time Bomb

Riots in the street
like in sixty-nine
Rampant revolution
is the talk of the time

We're getting really old
but we're making lots of clones
My only real hope is
I'm not going to survive it

We may have made it to the millennium
but I can't see making two thousand and one

It's a time bomb ticking down
Ticking down
A time bomb ticking down

No one could believe
we saw eighty-four
Forgot about big brother
now he's knocking at the door

Caught in the net
What did you expect
Maybe I could go
to Barcelona

I can't believe we made it this far
and now they want to send people to Mars

Last Day on Earth

Bob's been knockin'
and I'm just rockin'
Not giving a thought to my mortality

I've been blinded
Now I'm reminded
of life's eventual finality

Seems like thirty was only yesterday
I never dreamed that I'd have hell to pay

Live like it's your last day on earth
There's no telling what it might be worth
Who knows who might have been cursed
or when your bubble is about to burst
So live like it's your last day on earth

I'm just saying
cause the fabric's been fraying
A rent in my reality

No more ignoring
No saving no storing
Just mending my mentality

Every time the rain comes pouring down
I look for Noah just a hanging 'round

Acknowledgements

For me songwriting, unlike writing poetry, has always been a collaborative effort, since I write predominately lyrics.

All of the songs in this book were written with other people who collaborated with me with the music and sometimes with words or titles or ideas. It's been one of the great joys of my life. I've done my best to remember all of these friends but since some of the songs were written years ago I may not have remembered them all. I'm sorry if I left some names out. Please let me know if you are one of these and I'll put your name in the next edition.

Thanks
Fee

Gary Burr, Gary Cambra, David Foster, Bruce Gaitsch, Tom Keane, Pat Leonard, Steve Lukather, Richard Marx, Prairie Prince, Roger Steen.

Heart Trails

Hope you had a good day
Hope your heart
showed you the way
My heart will shepherd you
through the fray
And guide you back into my arms
I pray

Made in the USA
San Bernardino, CA
29 May 2015